BMP3

Best Management Practices to
Deter Piracy off the Coast of
Somalia and in the Arabian Sea Area

(Version 3 – June 2010)

Suggested Planning and Operational Practices for Ship Operators, and Masters of Ships Transiting the Gulf of Aden and the Arabian Sea

First Printed June 2010
ISBN 978 1 85609 397 2

Terms of Use

The advice and information given in this booklet ("Booklet") is intended purely as guidance to be used at the user's own risk. No warranties or representations are given nor is any duty of care or responsibility accepted by the Authors, their membership or employees of any person, firm, corporation or organisation (who or which has been in any way concerned with the furnishing of information or data, the compilation or any translation, publishing, supply of the Booklet) for the accuracy of any information or advice given in the Booklet or any omission from the Booklet or for any consequence whatsoever resulting directly or indirectly from compliance with, adoption of or reliance on guidance contained in the Booklet even if caused by a failure to exercise reasonable care on the part of any of the aforementioned parties.

Printed & bound in Great Britain by Bell & Bain Ltd. Glasgow

Published in 2010 by
Witherby Seamanship International Ltd,
4 Dunlop Square, Livingston,
Edinburgh, EH54 8SB,
Scotland, UK

Tel No: +44(0)1506 463 227
Email: info@emailws.com
www.witherbyseamanship.com

Contents

Section 1	Introduction	1
Section 2	Somali Pirate Activity	3
Section 3	Risk Assessment	5
Section 4	Typical Pirate Attacks	9
Section 5	Implementing BMP	11
Section 6	Company Planning	13
Section 7	Masters' Planning	15
Section 8	Prior to Transit – Voyage Planning	17
Section 9	Prior to Transit – Self Protection Measures	21
Section 10	If a Pirate Attack is Imminent	35
Section 11	If Boarded by Pirates	39
Section 12	In the Event of Military Action	41
Section 13	Post Incident Reporting	43
Section 14	Updating Best Management Practices	45
ANNEX A	Useful Contact Details	47
ANNEX B	UKMTO Vessel Position Reporting Form	48

ANNEX C	Piracy Definitions	49
ANNEX D	Follow-up Report	52
ANNEX E	Additional Guidance for Vessels Engaged in Fishing, in the Gulf of Aden and off the Coast of Somalia	55
ANNEX F	Organisations	59

Section 1

Introduction

1.1 The purpose of the Industry Best Management Practices (BMP) contained in this booklet is to assist ships to avoid, deter or delay piracy attacks off the coast of Somalia, including the Gulf of Aden (GoA) and the Arabian Sea area. Experience, supported by data collected by Naval forces, shows that the application of the recommendations contained within this booklet can and will make a significant difference in preventing a ship becoming a victim of piracy.

1.2 For the purposes of the BMP the term 'piracy' includes all acts of violence against ships, her crew and cargo. This includes armed robbery and attempts to board and take control of the ship, wherever this may take place.

1.3 Where possible, this booklet should be read with reference to the Maritime Security Centre – Horn of Africa website (www.mschoa.org), which provides additional and updating advice.

1.4 This BMP3 booklet updates the guidance contained within the 2nd edition of the Best Management Practice document published in August 2009.

1.5 This booklet complements piracy guidance provided in the latest IMO MSC Circulars

> **IMPORTANT: The extent to which the guidance given in this booklet is followed is always to be at the discretion of the Ship Operator and Master.**

Section 2

Somali Pirate Activity – The High Risk Area

2.1 The significant increase in the presence of Naval forces in the Gulf of Aden, concentrated on the Internationally Recommended Transit Corridor (IRTC), has significantly reduced the incidents of piracy attack in this area. With Naval forces concentrated in this area, Somali pirate activity has been forced from the Gulf of Aden out into the Arabian Sea. It is important to note, however, that there remains a serious threat from piracy in the Gulf of Aden.

2.2 Somali based pirate attacks have taken place both close to land and at extreme range from the Somali coast, and continue to do so.

2.3 The **High Risk Area** for piracy attacks defines itself by where the piracy attacks have taken place. For the purposes of the BMP, this is an **area bounded by Suez to the North, 10°S and 78°E**. While to date attacks have not been reported to the extreme East of this area, they have taken place at almost 70°E There remains the possibility that piracy attacks will take place even further to the East of the High Risk Area. Attacks have occurred to the extreme South of the High Risk Area. A high state of readiness and vigilance should be maintained even to the South of the Southerly limit of the High Risk Area and the latest advice from MSCHOA on the extent of pirate activity always sought (contact details are contained in Annex A). **It is recommended that the BMP is applied throughout the High Risk Area**.

Section 3
Risk Assessment

3.1 Prior to transiting the High Risk Area, Ship Operators and Masters should carry out a risk assessment to assess the likelihood and consequences of piracy attacks to the vessel, based on the latest available information (see Annex A for useful contacts, including MSCHOA and UKMTO). The output of this risk assessment should identify measures for prevention, mitigation and recovery, which will mean combining statutory regulations with supplementary measures to combat piracy.

Factors to be considered in the risk assessment should include, but may not be limited to, the following:

3.2 **Crew Safety:** The primary consideration should be to ensure the safety of the crew. Care should be taken, when formulating measures to prevent illegal boarding and external access to the accommodation, that crew members will not be trapped inside and should be able to escape in the event of another type of emergency, such as, for example fire.

3.3 **Freeboard:** It is likely that pirates will try to board the ship being attacked at the lowest point above the waterline, making it easier for them to climb onboard. These points are often on either quarter. Experience suggests that vessels with a minimum freeboard that is greater than 8 metres have a much greater chance of successfully escaping a piracy attempt than those with less. A large freeboard will provide little or no protection if the construction of the ship provides assistance to pirates seeking to climb onboard.

A large freeboard alone may not be enough to deter a pirate attack.

3.4 **Speed:** One of the most effective ways to defeat a pirate attack is by using speed to try to outrun the attackers and/or make it difficult to board. To date, there have been no reported attacks where pirates have boarded a ship that has been proceeding at over 18 knots. It is possible however that pirate tactics and techniques may develop to enable them to board faster moving ships. **Ships are recommended to proceed at Full Sea Speed in the High Risk Area**. If a vessel is part of a 'Group Transit' (see section 8.3 on page 17 for further details of Group Transits) within the International Recommended Transit Corridor (IRTC), speed may be required to be adjusted.

In the Gulf of Aden, ships capable of proceeding in excess of 18 knots are strongly recommended to do so. Within the remainder of the High Risk Area ships are reminded that speed is extremely important in avoiding or deterring a pirate attack. It is recommended that reference should be made to the MSCHOA website for the latest threat guidance regarding pirate attack speed capability.

3.5 **Sea State:** Pirates mount their attacks from very small craft, even where they are supported by larger vessels or 'mother ships', which tends to limit their operations to moderate sea states. While no statistics exist, it is likely to be more difficult to operate these small craft effectively in sea state 3 and above.

3.6 **Pirate Activity:** The risk of a piracy attack appears to increase immediately following the release of a hijacked vessel and/or following a period of poor weather when pirates have been unable to operate.

8

Section 4

Typical Pirate Attacks

4.1 Commonly, two or more small high speed (up to 25 knots) open boats or 'skiffs' are used in attacks, often approaching from either quarter or the stern. Pirates appear to favour trying to board ships from the port quarter.

4.2 The use of a pirate 'mother ship', carrying personnel, equipment, supplies and smaller attack craft, has enabled attacks to be undertaken at a greater range from the shore. Pirates are also using larger long range attack craft to attack at much greater distance from the Somali Coast.

4.3 Somali pirates seek to place their skiffs alongside the ship being attacked to enable one or more armed pirates to climb onboard. Pirates frequently use long lightweight ladders to climb up the side of the vessel being attacked. Once onboard the pirate (or pirates) will generally make their way to the bridge to take control of the vessel. Once on the bridge the pirate/pirates will demand that the ship slows/stops to enable further pirates to board.

4.4 Attacks have taken place at most times of the day. However, many pirate attacks have taken place early in the morning, at first light. Attacks have occurred at night, but this is less common.

4.5 It is not uncommon for pirates to use small arms fire and Rocket Propelled Grenades (RPGs) in an effort to intimidate Masters of ships to reduce speed and stop to allow the pirates to board. In what are difficult circumstances, it is very important to maintain Full Sea Speed, increasing speed where possible, and using careful manoeuvring to resist the attack.

4.6 The majority of attempted hijacks have been repelled by ship's crew who have planned and trained in advance of the passage and applied the BMPs contained within this booklet.

Section 5

Implementing BMP

5.1 Not all measures discussed in this booklet may be applicable for every ship type. Therefore, as part of the Risk Assessment, it is important to determine which of the BMP will be most suitable for individual ships.

5.2 An essential part of BMP that applies to all ships is liaison with Naval forces. This is to ensure that Naval forces are aware of the sea passage that a ship is about to embark upon and how vulnerable that ship is to pirate attack. This information is essential to enable the Naval forces to best use the assets available to them. Once ships have commenced passage it is important that they continue to update the Naval forces on progress. The three key Naval organisations to contact are:

    5.2.1 The Maritime Security Centre – Horn of Africa (MSCHOA) is the planning and coordination authority for EU forces (EU NAVFOR) in the Gulf of Aden and the Somalia Basin. (See contact details at Annex A.)

    5.2.2 UKMTO is the first point of contact for ships in the region. The day-to-day interface between Masters and Naval forces is provided by UKMTO, who talk to the ships and liaise directly with MSCHOA and the Naval commanders at sea. UKMTO require regular updates on the position and intended movements of ships. They use this information to help the Naval units maintain an accurate picture of shipping. (See contact details at Annex A). A copy of the UKMTO Vessel Position Reporting Form is attached at Annex B.

    5.2.3 The Martime Liaison Office Bahrain (MARLO) operates as a conduit for information exchange between the Combined Maritime Forces (CMF) and industry within the region. (See contact details at Annex A).

12

Section 6

Company Planning

6.1 It is strongly recommended that ship operators register for access to the restricted sections of the MSCHOA website (www.mschoa.org) prior to entering the High Risk Area as it contains additional and updated information.

6.2 On entering the UKMTO Voluntary Reporting Area (or High Risk Area) – an area bounded by Suez to the North, 10°S and 78°E – ensure that a UKMTO Vessel Position Reporting Form is sent (this can be done by either the ship or ship operator).

6.3 4-5 days before the vessel enters the International Recommended Transit Corridor (IRTC), ensure that a 'Vessel Movement Registration Form' has been submitted to MSCHOA (either on line, by email or by fax –see contact details at Annex A)

6.4 Review the Ship Security Assessment (SSA) and implementation of the Ship Security Plan (SSP), as required by the **International Ship and Port Facility Security Code** (ISPS), to counter the piracy threat, including the addition of UKMTO (as a recognised emergency response authority), as an SSAS recipient.

6.5 The Company Security Officer (CSO) is encouraged to see that a contingency plan is in place for a passage through the High Risk Area, and that this is exercised, briefed and discussed with the Master and the Ship Security Officer (SSO).

6.6 Be aware of any specific threats within the High Risk Areas that have been promulgated (by for example Navigational Warnings on SAT C or alerts on the MSCHOA website – www.mschoa.org.

6.7 Offer the Ship's Master guidance with regard to the recommended routeing through the High Risk Area and available methods of transiting the IRTC (eg Group Transit or national convoy where these exist). Reference should be made to the MSCHOA website for the latest routeing guidance (see contact details at Annex A).

6.8 Conduct crew training sessions prior to transits and debriefing sessions post transits.

6.9 The provision of carefully planned and installed **Self Protection Measures** (SPMs) prior to transiting the High Risk Area is very strongly recommended. Suggested SPMs are set out within this booklet. The use of SPMs significantly increases the prospects of a ship resisting a pirate attack.

6.10 Consider additional resources to enhance watch-keeping numbers.

6.11 The use of additional private security guards is at the discretion of the company, but the use of armed guards is not recommended.

Section 7

Masters' Planning

7.1 On entering the UKMTO Voluntary Reporting Area (or High Risk Area) – an area bounded by Suez to the North, 10°S and 78°E – ensure that a UKMTO Vessel Position Reporting Form is sent (this can be done by either the ship or ship operator).

7.2 4-5 days before the vessel enters the Internationally Recommended Transit Corridor (IRTC) ensure that a 'Vessel Movement Registration Form' has been submitted to MSCHOA (either online, by email or fax – see contact details at Annex A).

7.3 Prior to entry into the High Risk Area it is recommended that the crew should be briefed on the preparations and a drill conducted prior to arrival in the area. The plan should be reviewed and all personnel briefed on their duties, including familiarity with the alarm signal signifying a piracy attack, an all clear and the appropriate response to each.

7.4 Masters are advised to also prepare an emergency communication plan, to include all essential emergency contact numbers and prepared messages, which should be ready at hand or permanently displayed near the communications panel (eg telephone numbers of MSCHOA, IMB, PRC, CSO etc – see list of Contacts at Annex A).

7.5 Define the ship's AIS policy: The Master has the discretion to switch off the AIS if he believes that its use increases the ship's vulnerability. To provide Naval forces with tracking information within the Gulf of Aden it is recommended that AIS transmission is left on, but is restricted to ship's identity, position, course, speed, navigational status and safety-related information. Outside of the Gulf of Aden, in other parts of the

High Risk Area, the decision on AIS policy is again left to the Master's discretion, but current Naval advice is to turn it off completely. If in doubt this can be verified with MSCHOA.

7.6 If the AIS is switched off it should be activated at the time of an attack.

Section 8

Prior to Transit – Voyage Planning

8.1 Vessels are encouraged to report their noon position, course, speed, and destination to UKMTO while operating in the Voluntary Reporting Area, which is also the High Risk Area, using the UKMTO Vessel Position Reporting Form (see Annex B).

8.2 Vessels are also encouraged to increase the frequency of such reports to six hourly intervals when within six hours of entering or navigating within the IRTC.

8.3 Inside the Gulf of Aden

i. It is strongly recommended that ships navigate within the IRTC, where Naval forces are concentrated. Westbound ships should navigate to the northern part portion of the corridor, and eastbound ships should navigate in the southern part of the IRTC.

ii. Naval Forces, coordinated by MSCHOA, operate the 'Group Transit' scheme within the IRTC. This scheme groups vessels together by speed for maximum protection for their transit through the IRTC. Further guidance on the Group Transit scheme, including the departure timings for the different groups, are included on the MSCHOA website or can be obtained by fax from MSCHOA (see contact details at Annex A). Use of the Group Transit scheme is recommended. Masters should note that warships might not be within visual range of the ships in the Group Transit, but this does not lessen the protection afforded by the scheme.

iii. Ships may be asked to make adjustments to passage plans to conform to MSCHOA routeing advice. Ships joining a Group Transit should:

- Carefully time their arrival to avoid a slow speed approach to the forming up point (Point A or B)
- avoid waiting at the forming up point (Point A or B).
- Note that ships are particularly vulnerable to a pirate attack if they slowly approach or wait at the forming up points (Points A&B).

iv. Ships should avoid entering Yemeni Territorial Waters (12 miles) while on transit as it is not possible for international Naval forces (non-Yemeni) to protect ships that are attacked inside Yemeni Territorial Waters.

8.4 The High Risk Area (Outside the Gulf of Aden)

  i. Great care should be taken in voyage planning in the High Risk Area given that pirate attacks are taking place at extreme range from the Somali Coast. It is important to obtain the latest information from MSCHOA before planning and executing a voyage. Details can be obtained from the MSCHOA website or by fax (see contact details at Annex A).

  ii. Masters should update UKMTO on their intended movements using the UKMTO Vessel Position Reporting Form (see Annex B).

20

Section 9

Prior to Transit - Self Protection Measures

9.1 The guidance within this section primarily focuses on preparations that might be within the capability of the ship's crew, using equipment that will normally be readily available. The guidance is based on experience of piracy attacks to date and may require amendment over time if the pirates change their methods. Owners of vessels that make frequent transits through the High Risk Area may consider making further alterations to the vessel beyond the scope of this booklet, and/or provide additional equipment, and/or manpower as a means of further reducing the risk of piracy attack.

9.2 Watchkeeping and Enhanced Vigilance

Prior to commencing transit of the High Risk Area, it is recommended that preparations are made to support the requirement for increased vigilance by:

- Making arrangements to ensure additional lookouts for each Watch. Additional lookouts should be fully briefed.
- ensuring that there are sufficient binoculars for the enhanced bridge team
- considering night vision optics, if available.

Well constructed dummies placed at strategic locations around the vessel can give an impression of greater numbers of people on watch.

9.3 Closed Circuit Television (CCTV)

Once an attack is underway and pirates are firing weaponry at the vessel, it is difficult and dangerous to observe whether the pirates have managed to gain access. The use of CCTV coverage allows a degree of monitoring of the progress of the attack from a less exposed position:

- Consider the use of CCTV cameras to ensure coverage of vulnerable areas, particularly the poop deck
- consider positioning CCTV monitors at the rear of the bridge in a protected position

- further CCTV monitors could be located at the Safe Muster Point/Citadel (see page 33)
- recorded CCTV footage may provide useful evidence after an attack.

9.4 Manoeuvring Practice

> **Where navigationally safe to do so, Masters are encouraged to practice manoeuvring their ships to establish which series of helm orders produce the most difficult sea conditions for pirate skiffs trying to attack, without causing a significant reduction in the ship's speed.**

9.5 Alarms

Sounding the ship's alarms/whistle serves to inform the vessel's crew that a piracy attack has commenced and, importantly, demonstrates to any potential attacker that the ship is aware of the attack and is reacting to it. It is important to ensure that:

- The Piracy Alarm is distinctive to avoid confusion with other alarms, potentially leading to the crew mustering at the wrong location outside the accommodation
- crew members are familiar with each alarm, including the signal warning of an attack and an all clear, and the appropriate response to it
- exercises are carried out prior to entering the High Risk Area.

9.6 Upper Deck Lighting

It is recommended that the following lights are available and tested:

- Weather deck lighting around the accommodation block and rear facing lighting on the poop deck, consistent with

Rule 20(b) of the International Regulations for the Preventing Collision at Sea.

- search lights for immediate use when required
- it is, however, recommended that ships proceed with just their navigation lights illuminated, with the lighting described above extinguished. Once pirates have been identified or an attack commences, illuminating the lighting described above demonstrates to the pirates that they have been observed.

> **Navigation lights should not be switched off at night.**

9.7 Deny Use of Ship's Tools and Equipment

Pirates generally board vessels with little in the way of equipment other than personal weaponry. It is important to try to deny pirates the use of ship's tools or equipment that may be used to gain entry into the superstructure of the vessel. Tools and equipment that may be of use to the pirates should be stored in a secure location.

9.8 Protection of Equipment Stored on the Upper Deck

Small arms and other weaponry are often directed at the vessel and are particularly concentrated on the bridge, accommodation section and poop deck.

- Consideration should be given to providing protection, in the form of sandbags or Kevlar blankets, to gas bottles (ie oxy-acetylene) or containers of flammable liquids that must be stored in these locations
- ensure that any excess gas bottles or flammable materials are landed prior to transit.

9.9 Control of Access to Accommodation and Machinery Spaces

It is very important to control access routes to deter or delay pirates who have managed to board a vessel and are trying to enter accommodation or machinery spaces.

- All doors and hatches providing access to the accommodation and machinery spaces should be secured to prevent them being opened by pirates gaining access to the upper deck of the vessel
- careful consideration should be given to the means of securing doors and hatches
- it is recommended that once doors and hatches are secured, a designated and limited number are used for routine access when required, as controlled by the Officer of the Watch
- consideration should be given to blocking or lifting external ladders on the accommodation block to prevent their use and to restrict external access to the bridge
- where the door or hatch is located on an escape route from a manned compartment, it is essential that it can be opened by a seafarer trying to effect an exit by that route. Where the door or hatch is locked it is essential that a key is available, in a clear position by the door or hatch
- where doors and hatches are required to be closed for watertight integrity, ensure all clips are fully dogged down in addition to any locks.

9.10 Enhanced Bridge Protection

Further protection against flying glass can be provided by fitting security glass film

The bridge is usually the focus for the attack. In the initial part of the attack, pirates direct weapons fire at the bridge to try to coerce the ship to stop. Once onboard the vessel they usually try to make for the bridge to enable them to take control. Consideration of the following further protection enhancements might be considered:

- Kevlar jackets and helmets available for the bridge team to provide a level of protection for those on the bridge during an attack. (If possible, jackets and helmets should be in a non-military colour)
- while most bridge windows are laminated, further protection against flying glass can be provided by the application of security glass film
- fabricated metal (steel/aluminium) plates for the side and rear bridge windows and the bridge wing door windows, which may be rapidly secured in place in the event of an attack
- the after part of both bridge wings (often open) can be protected by a wall of sandbags.

9.11 Physical Barriers

Pirates typically use ladders and grappling hooks with rope attached to board vessels underway, so physical barriers should be used to make this difficult. Before constructing any physical barriers it is recommended that a survey is conducted to identify areas vulnerable to pirates trying to gain access; this may require constructing significant lengths of barriers to protect the ship. A robust razor wire barrier is particularly effective if constructed outboard of, or overhanging, the ship's structure so as to make it difficult for pirates to hook on their boarding ladder (or grappling hook) to the ship's structure.

- Razor wire (also known as barbed tape) creates an effective barrier when carefully deployed. The barbs on the wire are designed to have a piercing and gripping action. Care should be taken when selecting appropriate razor wire as the quality (wire gauge and frequency of barbs) and type will vary considerably. Lower quality razor wire is likely to be less effective. Three main types of razor wire are commonly available – Unclipped (straight strand), Spiral (like a telephone cord) and Concertina (linked spirals). Concertina razor wire is recommended as the linked spirals make it the most effective barrier. Razor wire should be constructed of high tensile wire, which is difficult to cut with hand tools. Concertina razor wire coil diameters of approximately 730 mm or 980 mm are recommended.

- It is important that the razor wire is properly secured and it is recommended that clips or wire ties are used every 50 cm, alternating between the upper and lower strands. Try not to leave gaps in the razor wire coverage as these are likely to be exploited by pirates. A double roll of Concertina razor wire provides a very effective barrier. When deploying razor wire personal protective equipment to protect hands, arms and faces must be used. Moving razor wire using wire hooks (like meat hooks) rather that by gloved hand reduces the risk of injury. It is recommended that razor wire is provided in shorter sections (eg 10metre section) as it is significantly easier and safer to use than larger sections which can be very heavy and unwieldy.
- coating gunwhales and other potentially vulnerable structures with 'anti-climb' paint may also be considered
- electrified barriers are not recommended for hydrocarbon carrying vessels, but following a safety assessment can be appropriate and effective for some other types of vessel

- it is recommended that warning signs of the electrified fence or barrier are displayed - inward facing in English/language of the crew, outward facing in Somali
- the use of such outward facing warning signs might also be considered even if no part of the barrier is actually electrified.

KHATAR

Deyr Danab Koronto Sare (Xooggan)

Example of a warning sign in Somali, which states –
DANGER HIGH VOLTAGE ELECTRIC BARRIER

9.12 Water Spray and Foam Monitors

The use of water spray and/or foam monitors has been found to be effective in deterring or delaying pirates attempting to board a vessel. The use of water can make it difficult for a pirate skiff to remain alongside and makes it significantly more difficult for a pirate to try to climb onboard.

Picture courtesy of NATO (2008)

Manual operation of hoses and foam monitors is not recommended as this is likely to place the operator in a particularly exposed position.

- It is recommended that hoses and foam monitors (delivering water) should be fixed in position to cover likely pirate access routes. Some ships have used spray rails using a GRP(Glass Reinforced Plastic) water main, with spray nozzles to produce a water curtain to cover larger areas

- heating the water used to deter pirates has also been found to be very effective in deterring attacks
- once rigged and fixed in position it is recommended that hoses and foam monitors are in a ready state, requiring just the remote activation of fire pumps to commence delivery of water. Actual foam supply should not be used (unless an additional quantity for this specific purpose is carried) as this will be depleted relatively quickly and will leave the vessel exposed in the event that the foam supply is required for firefighting purposes
- observe the water and foam monitor spray achieved by the equipment, once fixed in position, to ensure effective coverage of vulnerable areas
- improved water coverage may be achieved by using baffle plates fixed a short distance in front of the nozzle.

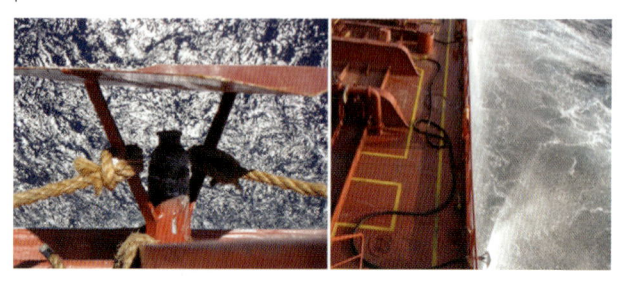

9.13 Safe Muster Points/Citadels

Any decision to navigate in areas where the vessel's security may be threatened requires careful consideration and detailed planning to best ensure the safety of the vessel and crew. Consider establishing either an internal 'Safe Muster Point' or a secure 'Citadel'. The guidelines for each are as follows:

(i) Safe Muster Point Guidelines:

A safe muster station is a designated area chosen to provide maximum physical protection to the crew. In the event of a pirate attack, those members of the crew not required on the bridge or MCR will muster. A Safe Muster Point is a short-term safe haven.

(ii) Citadel Guidelines:

A Citadel is a designated pre-planned area purpose built into the ship where, in the event of imminent boarding by pirates, all crew will seek protection. A Citadel is designed and constructed to resist a determined pirate trying to gain entry. Such a space would probably have, but not be limited to, its own self-contained air-conditioning, emergency rations, water supply, good external communications, emergency shut-down capability for the main and auxiliary engines, and remotely operated CCTV cameras.

A Citadel is to provide longer term protection of the crew.

> **Ship Operators and Masters are strongly advised to check directly with MSCHOA regarding the use of Citadels (see contact details in Annex A).**

The whole concept of the Citadel approach is lost if any crew member is left outside before it is secured.

34

Section 10

If a Pirate Attack is Imminent

10.1 Follow the ship's pre-prepared contingency plan.

10.2 Activate the Emergency Communication Plan and report the attack immediately to the single primary point of contact in the event of an attack, which is UKMTO. (MSCHOA acts as a back-up contact point in the event of an attack).

10.3 Activate the Ship Security Alert System (SSAS), which will alert your Company Security Officer and Flag State. Post-attack reports should be communicated as quickly as possible to contacts listed at Annex A using the report form in Annex C.

10.4 If the Master has exercised his right to turn off the Automatic Identification System (AIS) during transit of the piracy area, this should be turned on once the ship comes under pirate attack.

10.5 Sound the emergency alarm and make a 'pirate attack' (PA) announcement in accordance with the ship's emergency plan.

10.6 Make a 'Mayday' call on VHF Ch. 16 (and backup Ch. 08, which is monitored by naval units). Send a distress message via the DSC (Digital Selective Calling) system and Inmarsat-C, as applicable. Establish telephone communication with UKMTO.

10.7 Prevent skiffs closing on the ship by altering course and increasing speed where possible. Pirates have great difficulty boarding a ship that is:

1. Making way at over 18 knots.

2. Manoeuvring – it is recommended that, as early as possible, Masters undertake continuous small zigzag manoeuvres to further deter boarding while maintaining speed. Consider increasing the pirates' exposure to wind/waves and using bow wave and stern wash to restrict pirate craft coming alongside. (Masters and the Officer of the Watch should be fully familiar with the handling and manoeuvring characteristics of the vessel and should not wait until attacked to practice their evasive maneuvering techniques). Particular attention should be given to the effects of varying helm orders and the impact these can have on the ship's speed.

3. Activate water and spray and other appropriate defensive measures.

10.8 All crew who are not involved in counter-piracy operations should be mustered, either at their designated Safe Muster Point, or the Citadel if the ship is appropriately constructed.

Section 11
If Boarded by Pirates

11.1 Try to remain calm.

11.2 Before the pirates gain access to the bridge, inform UKMTO and, if time permits, the Company.

11.3 Offer no resistance to the pirates once they reach the bridge. Once on the bridge the pirates are likely to be highly agitated, so remaining calm and cooperating fully will greatly reduce the risk of harm.

11.4 If the bridge/engine room is to be evacuated the main engine should be stopped all way taken off the vessel if possible, and the ship navigated clear of other ships. All remaining crew members should proceed to the designated Safe Muster Point with their hands visible and on their heads.

11.5 If the ship is constructed with a Citadel and the Ship's Security Plan (SSP) involves the evacuation of all persons to the Citadel, ensure that the main engine is stopped, the vessel has adequate sea room to drift and the Citadel space is properly secured.

11.6 Owners and Seafarers are reminded that they should check directly with MSCHOA regarding the latest guidance regarding the use of Citadels. Irrespective of the latest guidance it should be remembered that the whole concept of a Citadel approach is lost if any crew member is left outside before it is secured.

11.7 Leave any CCTV running.

DO NOT use firearms, even if available.

DO NOT make any sudden movements around pirates.

DO NOT use flash photography.

DO NOT use flares of other pyrotechnics as weapons.

Section 12

In the Event of Military Action

12.1 In the event that military personnel take action onboard the ship, all personnel should keep low to the deck and cover their head with both hands, with hands visible.

12.2 Do not use flash photography.

12.3 Be prepared to be challenged on your identity. Brief and prepare ship's personnel to expect this and to cooperate fully during any military action onboard.

12.4 Be aware that English is not the working language of all Naval forces in the region.

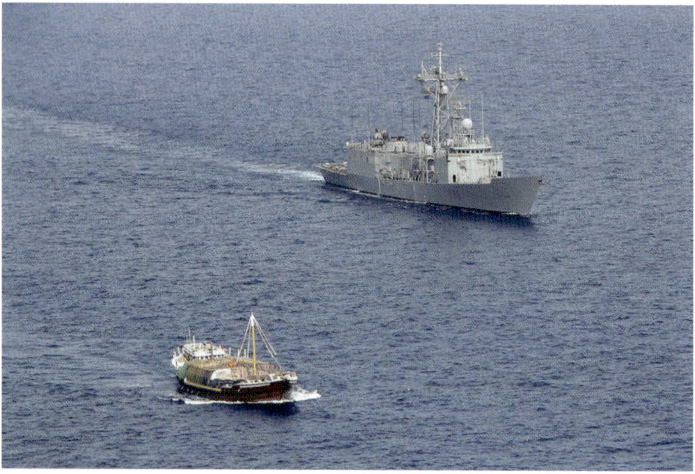

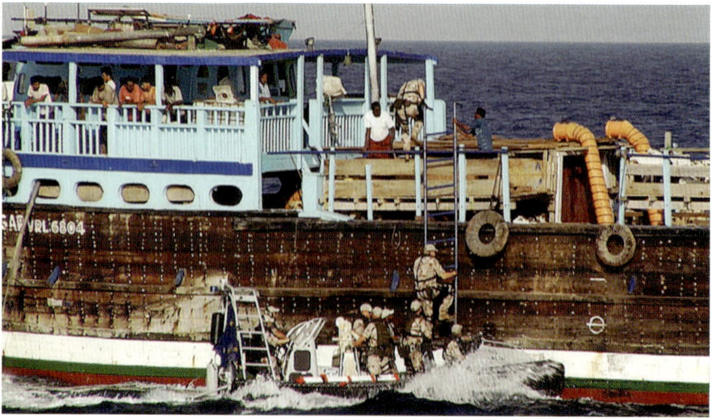
VRL 6804

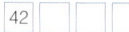

Section 13
Post Incident Reporting

13.1 Following any piracy attack or suspicious activity, it is vital that a detailed report of the event is reported to UKMTO, MSCHOA, and the IMB.

13.2 This will ensure full analysis and trends in piracy activity are established and will enable assessment of piracy techniques or changes in tactics, in addition to ensuring appropriate warnings can be issued to other Merchant shipping in the vicinity.

13.3 Masters are, therefore, requested to complete the standardised piracy report form contained in Annex D.

13.4 Ship Operators and Masters are also encouraged to forward a copy of the completed standardised piracy report (contained in Annex D) to their Flag State.

Section 14

Updating Best Management Practices

14.1 The Industry Organisations engaged in producing this Booklet will endeavour to meet regularly and will ensure the BMPs are updated as necessary, based upon operational experience and lessons learned.

ANNEX A
Useful Contact Details

1) UKMTO

- Email: UKMTO@eim.ae
- Telephone: +971 50 552 3215

2) MSCHOA

- Via Website
  for reporting: www.mschoa.org
  Telephone: +44 (0) 1923 958545
- Fax: +44 (0) 1923 958520
- Email: postmaster@mschoa.org

3) NATO SHIPPING CENTRE

- Website: www.shipping.nato.int
- Email: info@shipping.nato.int
- Telephone: +44(0)1923 956574
- Fax: +44(0)1923 956575

4) MARLO

- Email: Marlo.bahrain@me.navy.mi
- Office: +973 1785 3925
- Duty (24hrs): +973 3940 1395

5) IMB

- Email: piracy@icc-ccs.org
- Telephone: +60 3 2031 0014
- Fax: +60 3 2078 5769
- Telex: MA34199 IMBPC1

ANNEX B

UKMTO Vessel Position Reporting Form

Masters and Owners should check with the MSCHOA website for the latest information regarding the UKMTO Voluntary reporting areas at http://www.mschoa.eu or with UKMTO.

UKMTO Vessel Position Reporting Form (*Transmit at least Once Daily*)

1	Ship Name	
2	Flag	
3	IMO Number	
4	INMARSAT Telephone Number	
5	Time & Position	
6	Course	
7	Passage Speed	
8	Freeboard	
9	Cargo	
10	Destination and Estimated Time of Arrival	
11	Name and contact details of Company Security Officer	
12	Nationality of Master and Crew	

ANNEX C
Piracy Definitions

1. It is important to try to harmonise common definitions and guidelines for Piracy attacks & suspicious activity because common reporting within the industry will ensure:

   1.1 Harmonised data assessment.

   1.2 Provision of consistent reporting.

   1.3 Harmonised Intelligence gathering.

   1.4 Better accuracy in assessing the efficiency of (Naval) counter piracy operations and BMP effectiveness as well as defining future end dates to operations.

2. 'Piracy' is defined in the 1982 United Nations Convention on the Law of the Sea (UNCLOS) (article 101). However, for the purposes of these BMP, it is important to provide clear, practical, working guidance to the Industry to enable accurate and consistent assessment, of suspicious activity and piracy attacks.

3. The following are the BMP Guidelines to assist in assessing what is a Piracy attack and what is suspicious activity

   3.1 A piracy attack may include (but is not limited to) actions such as the following:

   3.1.1 The use of violence against the ship or its personnel, or any attempt to use violence.

   3.1.2 Attempt(s) to board the vessel where the Master suspects the persons are pirates.

   3.1.3 An actual boarding whether successful in gaining control of the vessel or not.

3.1.4 Attempts to overcome the ship's self protection measures by the use of:
  i. Ladders.
  ii. Grappling hooks.
  iii. Weapons deliberately used against or at the vessel.

4. Guidelines for defining suspicious activity:

4.1 Action taken by another craft may be deemed suspicious if any of the following occur (the list is not exhaustive):

4.1.1 A definite course alteration towards the craft associated with a rapid increase in speed, by the suspected craft, which cannot be accounted for as normal activity in the circumstances prevailing in the area.

4.1.2 Small craft sailing on the same course and speed for an uncommon period and distance, not in keeping with normal fishing or other circumstances prevailing in the area.

4.1.3 Sudden changes in course towards the vessel and aggressive behavior.

5. Guidance Note:

5.1 In helping to evaluate suspicious activity, the following may be of assistance to determine the nature of a suspect vessel:

1. The number of crew on board relative to its size.

2. The Closest Point of Approach (CPA).

3. The existence of unusual and non-fishing equipment, eg ladders, climbing hooks or large amounts of fuel onboard.

4. If the craft is armed in excess of the level commonly experienced in the area.

5. If weapons are fired in the air.

5.2 This is not an exhaustive listing. Other events, activity and craft may be deemed suspicious by the Master of a merchant vessel having due regard to their own seagoing experiences within the High Risk Area or Gulf of Aden areas and information shared amongst the international maritime community. The examples above are to be treated only as guidance and are not definitive or exhaustive.

ANNEX D

Follow-up Report

PIRACY ATTACK REPORT VESSEL PARTICULARS/DETAILS:

1	Name of Ship:
2	IMO No:
3	Flag:
4	Call Sign:
5	Type of Ship:
6	Tonnages: GRT: NRT: DWT:
7	Owners (Address & Contact Details):
8	Managers (Address & Contact Details):
9	Last Port/Next Port:
10	Cargo Details: (Type/Quantity)

Details of Incident

11	Date & Time of Incident: LT UTC
12	Position: Lat: (N/S) Long: (E/W)
13	Nearest Land Mark/Location:
14	Port/Town/Anchorage Area:
15	Country/Nearest Country:
16	Status (Berth/Anchored/Steaming):
17	Own Ship's Speed:
18	Ship's Freeboard During Attack:
19	Weather During Attack (Rain/Fog/Mist/Clear/etc, Wind (Speed and Direction), Sea/Swell Height):
20	Types of Attack (Boarded/Attempted):
21	Consequences for Crew, Ship and Cargo: Any Crew Injured/Killed: Items/Cash Stolen:
22	Area of the Ship being Attacked:
23	Last Observed Movements of Pirates/Suspect Craft:

Details of Raiding Party

24	Number of Pirates/Robbers:
25	Dress/Physical Appearance:
26	Language Spoken:
27	Weapons Used:
28	Distinctive Details:
29	Craft Used:
30	Method of Approach:
31	Duration of Attack:
32	Aggressive/Violent:

Further Details

33	Action Taken by Master and Crew and its effectiveness:
34	Was Incident Reported to the Coastal Authority? If so to Whom?
35	Preferred Communications with Reporting Ship: Appropriate Coast Radio Station/HF/MF/VHF/INMARSAT IDS (Plus Ocean Region Code)/MMSI
36	Action Taken by the Authorities:
37	Number of Crew/Nationality:
38	Please **Attach** with this Report – A Brief Description/Full Report/Master – Crew Statement of the Attack/Photographs taken if any.
39	Details of Self Protection Measures.

ANNEX E

The following guidance for vessels engaged in fishing has been provided by the following national fishing industry associations:

OPAGAC – Organizacion de Productores Asociados de Grandes Atuneros Congeladores

ANABAC – Asociacion Nacional de Armadores de Buques Atuneros Congeladores

> **ADDITIONAL GUIDANCE FOR VESSELS ENGAGED IN FISHING, IN THE GULF OF ADEN AND OFF THE COAST OF SOMALIA**
>
> **I. RECOMMENDATIONS TO VESSELS IN FISHING ZONES**
>
> 1. Non-Somali fishing vessels should avoid operating or transiting within 200 nm of the coast of Somalia, irrespective of whether or not they had been issued with licenses to do so.
> 2. Do not start fishing operations when the radar indicates the presence of unidentified boats.
> 3. If polyester skiffs of a type typically used by pirates are sighted, move away from them at full speed, sailing into the wind and sea to make their navigation more difficult.
> 4. Avoid stopping at night, be alert and maintain bridge, deck and engine-room watch.
> 5. During fishing operations, when the vessel is more vulnerable, be alert and maintain radar watch in order to give maximum notice to the Authorities if an attack is in progress.
> 6. While navigating at night, use only the mandatory navigation and safety lights so as to prevent the glow of lighting attracting

pirates, who sometimes are in boats without radar and are just lurking around.

7. While the vessel is drifting while fishing at night, keep guard at the bridge on deck and in the engine-room. Use only mandatory navigation and safety lights.

8. The engine must be ready for an immediate start-up.

9. Keep away from unidentified ships.

10. Use VHF as little as possible to avoid being heard by pirates and to make location more difficult.

11. Activate the AIS when maritime patrol aircraft are operating in the area to facilitate identification and tracking.

II. IDENTIFICATION

1. Managers are strongly recommended to register their fishing vessels with MSCHOA for the whole period of activity off the coast of Somalia. This should include communicating a full list of the crewmen on board and their vessels' intentions, if possible.

2. Carry out training prior to passage or fishing operations in the area.

3. Whenever fishing vessels are equipped with VMS devices, their manager should provide MSCHOA with access to VMS data.

4. Fishing vessels should avoid sailing through areas where they have been informed that suspected pirate 'mother ships' have been identified and should use all means to detect, as soon as possible, any movement of large or small vessels that could be suspicious.

5. Fishing vessels should always identify themselves upon request from aircraft or ships from Operation ATALANTA or other international or national anti-piracy operation.

6. Military, merchant and fishing vessels should respond without delay to any identification request made by a fishing vessel being approached (to facilitate early action to make escape possible, especially if the vessel is fishing).

III. IN CASE OF ATTACK

1. In case of an attack or sighting a suspicious craft, warn the Authorities (UKMTO and MSCHOA) and the rest of the fleet.

2. Communicate the contact details of the second master of the vessel (who is on land) whose knowledge of the vessel could contribute to the success of a military intervention.

Recommendations only for Purse Seiners

3. Evacuate all personnel from the deck and the crow's nest.

4. If pirates have taken control of the vessel and the purse seine is spread out, encourage the pirates to allow the nets to be recovered. If recovery of the purse seine is allowed, follow the instructions for its stowage and explain the functioning of the gear to avoid misunderstanding.

ANNEX F
Organisations

i. BMP3 Signatories

BIMCO

BIMCO is an independent international shipping association, with a membership composed of ship owners, managers, brokers agents and many other stakeholders with vested interests in the shipping industry. The association acts on behalf of its global membership to promote higher standards and greater harmony in regulatory matters. It is a catalyst for the development and promotion of fair and equitable international shipping policy BIMCO is accredited as a Non-Governmental Organisation (NGO), holds observer status with a number of United Nations organs and is in close dialogue with maritime administrations regulatory institutions and other stakeholders within the EU the USA and Asia. The association provides one of the most comprehensive sources of practical shipping information and a broad range of advisory and consulting services to its members www.bimco.org

ICS International Chamber of Shipping

The International Chamber of Shipping (ICS) is the international trade association for merchant ship operators. ICS represents the collective views of the international industry from different nations, sectors and trades. ICS membership comprises national shipowners' associations representing over 75% of the world's merchant fleet. A major focus of ICS activity is the International Maritime Organization (IMO) the United Nations agency with responsibility for the safety of life at sea and the protection of the marine environment. ICS is heavily involved in a wide variety of areas including any technical, legal and operational matters affecting merchant ships. ICS is unique in that it represents the global interests of all the different trades in the industry: bulk carrier operators, tanker operators, passenger ship operators and container liner trades, including shipowners and third party ship managers.

IGP&I. (The International Group of P&I Clubs).

The thirteen principal underwriting member clubs of the International Group of P&I Clubs ('the Group') between them provide liability cover (protection and indemnity) for approximately 90% of the world's ocean-going tonnage. Each Group club is an independent, non-profit making mutual insurance association, providing cover for its ship-owner and charterer members against third party liabilities relating to the use and operation of ships. Each club is controlled by its members through a board of directors or committee elected from the membership Clubs cover a wide range of liabilities including personal injury to crew, passengers and others on board, cargo loss and damage, oil pollution, wreck removal and dock damage. Clubs also provide a wide range of services to their members on claims, legal issues and loss prevention, and often play a leading role in the management of casualties www.igpandi.org

IMB

ICC International Maritime Bureau

The main objective of the International Maritime Bureau's Piracy Reporting Centre (PRC) is to be the first point of contact for the shipmaster to report an actual or attempted attack or even suspicious movements thus initiating the process of response. The PRC raises awareness within the shipping industry, which includes the shipmaster, ship-owner, insurance companies, traders, etc, of the areas of high risk associated with piratical attacks or specific ports and anchorages associated with armed robberies on board ships. They work closely with various governments and law enforcement agencies, and are involved in information sharing in an attempt to reduce and ultimately eradicate piracy.

INTERCARGO

INTERCARGO is the short name for the International Association of Dry Cargo Ship-owners. Since 1980, it has represented the interests of owners, operators and managers of dry cargo shipping and works closely with the other international associations to promote a safe, high quality, efficient and profitable industry.

INTERTANKO

INTERTANKO is the International Association of Independent Tanker Owners INTERTANKO has been the voice of independent tanker owners since 1970, ensuring that the oil that keeps the world turning is shipped safely, responsibly and competitively. Membership is open to independent tanker owners and operators of oil and chemical tankers, i.e. non-oil companies and non-state controlled tanker owners, who fulfil the Association's membership criteria. Independent owners operate some 80% of the world's tanker fleet and the vast majority are INTERTANKO members. As of January 2010, the organisation had 250 members, whose combined fleet comprises some 3,050 tankers totalling 260 million dwt. INTERTANKO's associate membership stands at some 330 companies with an interest in shipping of oil and chemicals.
www.intertanko.com

INTERNATIONAL SHIPPING FEDERATION

The International Shipping Federation (ISF) is the principal international employers' organisation for the shipping industry, representing all sectors and trades. ISF membership comprises national shipowners' associations whose member shipping companies together operate 75% of the world's merchant tonnage and employ a commensurate proportion of the world's 1.25 million seafarers. Established in 1909, ISF is concerned with all labour affairs, manpower and training, and seafarers' health and welfare issues that may have an impact on international shipping.

ITF (International Transport Workers Federation)

ITF (International Transport Workers Federation) The International Transport Workers' Federation (ITF) is an international trade union federation of transport workers' unions. Any independent trade union with members in the transport industry is eligible for membership of the ITF. The ITF has been helping seafarers since 1896 and today represents the interests of seafarers worldwide, of whom over 600,000 are members of ITF affiliated unions. The ITF is working to improve conditions for seafarers of all nationalities and to ensure adequate regulation of the shipping industry to protect the interests and rights of the workers. The ITF helps crews regardless of their nationality or the flag of their ship.

IPTA — The International Parcel Tankers Association

The International Parcel Tankers Association was formed in 1987 to represent the interests of the specialised chemical/parcel tanker fleet and has since developed into an established representative body for ship owners operating IMO classified chemical/parcel tankers, being recognised as a focal point through which regulatory authorities and trade organisations may liaise with such owners. IPTA was granted consultative status as a Non-Governmental Organisation to the International Maritime Organization (IMO) in 1997 and is wholly supportive of the IMO as the only body to introduce and monitor compliance with international maritime legislation.

Joint Hull — JHC (Joint Hull Committee)

The Joint Hull Committee (JHC) was founded in 1910 and comprises underwriting representatives from both Lloyd's syndicates and the IUA company market. It discusses all matters connected with hull insurance, and represents the interests of those writing marine hull business within the London market. It liaises widely with the broad maritime sector. The JHC, from time to time, issues circulars to the market which are of relevance to the hull underwriting community and these may include new model wordings, information about developments in shipping, and notices of briefings.

Joint War Committee — JWC (Joint War Committee)

The Joint War Committee (JWC) comprises underwriting representatives from both Lloyd's syndicates and the IUA company market. It discusses all matters connected with hull war insurance, and represents the interests of those writing marine hull war business within the London market. JWC takes advice from independent security advisers and from time to time, issues updates to its published Listed Areas. These are the areas of perceived enhanced risk for those writing the range of perils insured in the war market where coverage may be arranged against the risks of confiscation, derelict weapons, piracy, strikes, terrorism and war.

OCIMF — Oil Companies International Marine Forum (OCIMF)

The Oil Companies International Marine Forum (OCIMF) is a voluntary association of oil companies having an interest in the shipment and terminalling of crude oil and oil products. Our mission is to be the foremost authority on the safe and environmentally responsible operation of oil tankers and terminals, promoting continuous improvement in standards of design and operation. www.ocimf.com

SIGTTO

(The Society of International Gas Tanker and Terminal Operators) was established in 1979 to encourage safe and responsible operation of liquefied gas tankers and marine terminals handling liquefied gas, to develop advice and guidance for best industry practice among its members and to promote criteria for best practice to all who either have responsibilities for, or an interest in, the continuing safety of gas tankers and terminals. The Society is registered as a 'not for profit' entity in Bermuda and is owned by its members who are predominately the owners of assets in the LPG/LNG ship and terminal business. The Society has observer status at the IMO. www.sigtto.org

ii. BMP3 is supported by:

EU NAVFOR. (The European Union Naval Force).

EUNAVFOR is the main coordinating authority which operates the Maritime Security Centre (Horn of Africa). Operation Atalanta includes the deployment of a major EU Naval Task Group into the region to improve maritime security off the Somali coast. Additionally the mission also encompasses a broad range of liaison, both regionally and with industry, to help establish best practices and to disseminate information through its 24/7 manned Maritime Security Centre-Horn of Africa (MSC-HOA) and through the website www.mschoa.org

Combined Maritime Forces (CMF)

Combined Maritime Forces is a 24 nation coalition committed to ensuring regional security. CMF operates In accordance with international law and relevant United Nations Security Council Resolutions and is supported by three distinct missions. Combined Task Force (CTF) 150 operates in the Red Sea, Gulf of Aden, Indian Ocean, Arabian Sea and the Gulf of Oman conducting Maritime Security Operations. CTF 151 operates in the Gulf of Aden and Somali Basin to deter, disrupt and suppress piracy, protecting the safe passage of maritime vessels of any nationality. CTF 152 operates in the Arabian Gulf conducting maritime security operations in conjunction with Gulf Cooperation Council (GCC) partners in order to prevent destabilizing activities. www.cusnc.navy.mil/cmf/cmf_command.html

MARLO The Maritime Liaison Office

The Maritime Liaison Office (MARLO) mission is to facilitate the exchange of information between the United States Navy, Combined Maritime Forces, and the commercial maritime community in the United States Central Command's (CENTCOM) Area of Responsibility. MARLO operates as a conduit for information focused on the safety and security of shipping and is committed to assisting all members of the commercial maritime community. To help combat piracy, MARLO serves as a secondary emergency point of contact for mariners in distress (after UKMTO) and also disseminates transit guidance to the maritime industry.

Maritime Security Centre Horn of Africa (MSCHOA)

The Maritime Security Centre – Horn of Africa (MSCHOA) aims to provide a service to mariners in the Gulf of Aden, the Somali Basin and off the Horn of Africa. It is a Coordination Centre dedicated to safeguarding legitimate freedom of navigation in the light of increasing risks of pirate attack against merchant shipping in the region, in support of the UN Security Council's Resolutions (UNSCR) 1814, 1816 and 1838. Through close dialogue with shipping companies, masters and other interested parties, MSCHOA will build up a picture of vulnerable shipping in these waters and their approaches. The Centre, which is manned by military and merchant navy personnel from several countries, will then coordinate with a range of military forces operating in the region to provide support and protection to mariners. There is a clear need to protect ships and their crews from illegitimate and dangerous attacks, safeguarding a key global trade route. www.mschoa.org

Operation Ocean Shield

Operation Ocean Shield is NATO's contribution to international efforts to combat piracy off the Horn of Africa. The operation develops a distinctive NATO role based on the broad strength of the Alliance by adopting a more comprehensive approach to counter-piracy efforts. NATO's counter piracy efforts focus on at-sea counter-piracy operations, support to the maritime community to take actions to reduce incidence of piracy, as well as regional-state counter-piracy capacity building. The operation is designed to complement the efforts of existing international organisations and forces operating in the area.

NATO Shipping Centre (NSC)

NATO Shipping Centre (NSC) provides the commercial link with NATO's Maritime Forces. The NSC is NATO's primary point of contact with the maritime community and is used by NATO as the tool for communicating and coordinating initiatives and efforts with other military actors (most notably UK MTO, MSCHOA and MARLO) as well as directly with the maritime community, and thereby supporting the overall efforts to reduce the incidence of piracy.
www.shipping.nato.int

UKMTO

(The UK Royal Navy's Maritime Trade Organisation)

The UK Maritime Trade Operations (UKMTO) office in Dubai acts as the primary point of contact for merchant vessels and liaison with military forces in the region. UKMTO also administers the Voluntary Reporting Scheme, under which merchant vessels are encouraged to send regular reports, providing their position/course/ speed and ETA at their next port while transiting the region bound by Suez, 78°E and 10°S. UKMTO subsequently tracks vessels and the positional information is passed to CMF and EU headquarters. Emerging and relevant information affecting commercial traffic can then be passed directly to ships, rather than by company offices, improving responsiveness to any incident and saving time. For further information or to join the Voluntary Reporting Scheme, please contact UKMTO or MSCHOA Email: ukmto@eim.ae

NOT TO BE USED FOR NAVIGATION

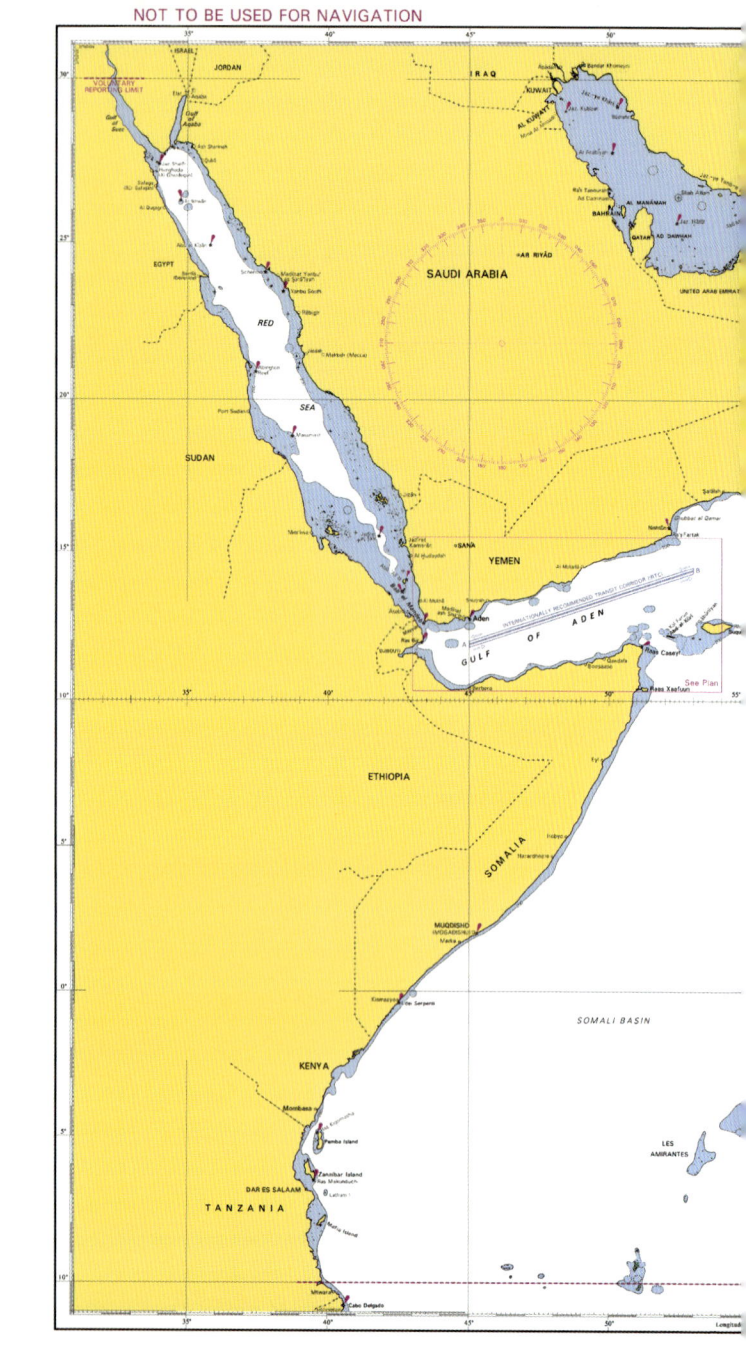

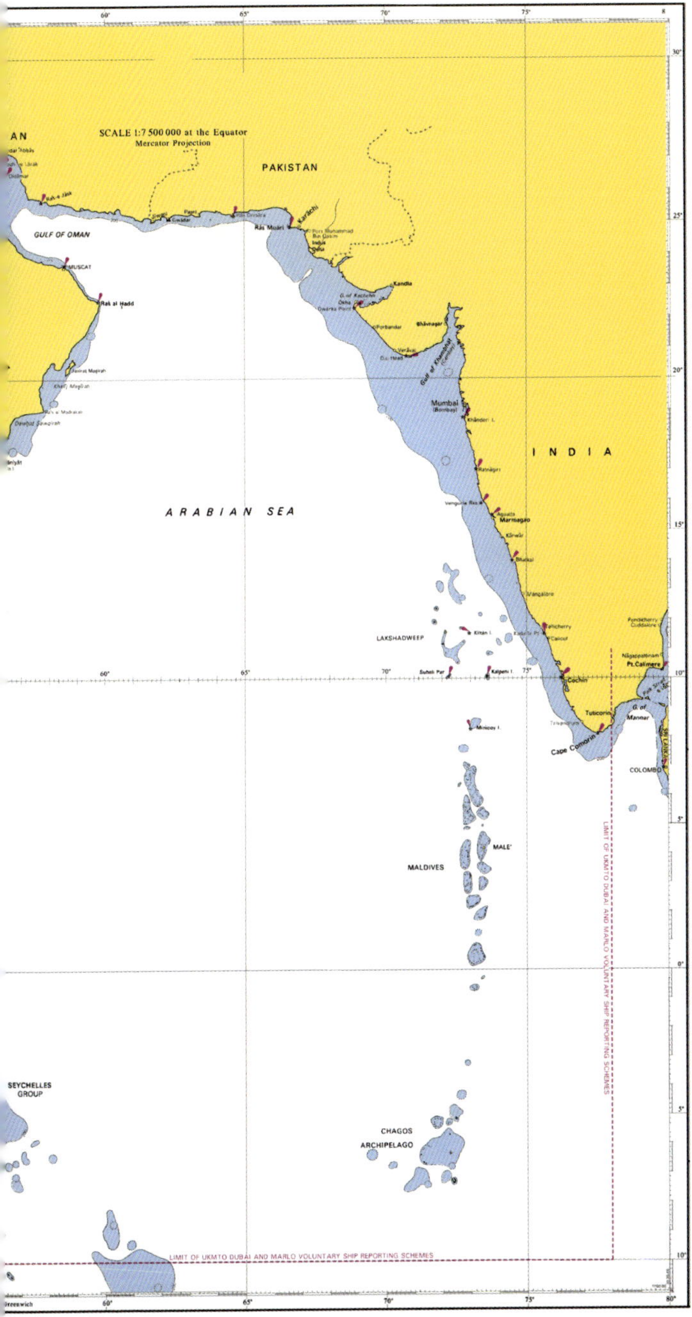
SCALE 1:7 500 000 at the Equator
Mercator Projection
PAKISTAN
INDIA
ARABIAN SEA
GULF OF OMAN
MUSCAT
Ras al Hadd
Karachi
Ras Muari
Gwadar
Kandla
G. of Kachchh
Okha
Dwarka Point
Porbandar
Bhavnagar
Gulf of Khambhat
Mumbai
(Bombay)
Ratnagiri
Vengurla Rks
Marmagao
Karwar
Bhatkal
Mangalore
Tellicherry
Calicut
Cochin
Tuticorin
Cape Comorin
G. of
Mannar
Pt.Calimere
COLOMBO
LAKSHADWEEP
Minicoy I.
MALDIVES
MALE'
CHAGOS
ARCHIPELAGO
SEYCHELLES
GROUP
LIMIT OF UKMTO DUBAI AND MARLO VOLUNTARY SHIP REPORTING SCHEMES
60°
65°
70°
75°
80°
30°
25°
20°
15°
10°
5°
0°
Greenwich